Wisdom For The New Believer

Wisdom For The New Believer:
Preparing new believers for a relationship with Jesus Christ.
Copyright @ 2020 James T Curtis
ISBN: 978-1-7349955-0-3
All rights reserved. No part of this book may be used or reproduced by any means without the permission of the author except in the case of brief quotations embodied in critical articles and reviews.

Scripture taken from the **King James Version**

Printed in the United States Of America

Wisdom For The New Believer

Preparing New Believers For A Relationship With Jesus Christ

By
James T Curtis

TABLE OF CONTENTS

Introduction

Chapter 1.
A New Creation In Christ……………………. 8

Chapter 2.
Baptized In The Holy Spirit………………….. 34

Chapter 3.
The Supernatural Is Your Reality…………….. 44

Chapter 4.
Take Up Your New Authority…………………. 66

Chapter 5.
Remaining In The Secret Place……………….. 72

Conclusion. Jesus, Jesus, Jesus………………...86

Introduction

It is my dearest hope that you are reading this book because you have recently dedicated your life or have rededicated your life to Jesus Christ. The greatest gift we can ever receive is the gift of eternal life and it's free! I have recognized that many born-again Christians have heard the calling of God in their life but they do not know how to move forward in their walk with Jesus.

In this book, I will give you first-hand insight on how to move forward in your new life as a born-again Christian. It is my hope that you can avoid some of the pitfalls that might come with being born-again. I pray that you take the teachings in this book and move forward with a great desire to read the Bible daily.

Wisdom For The New Believer

-Chapter One-
✝ A New Creation In Christ ✝

Therefore if any man be in Christ, he is a new creature: old things are passed away; behold, all things are become new.
2 Corinthians 5:17 KJV

Congratulations, you're dead! The old you has passed away and the new you has raised to life with Jesus Christ! The first thing you need to know is that *there was no possible way for you to become born again without hearing the voice of GOD!*

It's important you understand that you have now heard the voice of God and from this day forward his voice is only going to become easier for you to hear. God calls all people towards Him. You were predestined to become a son or daughter of God.

God called you to your new life in Christ long before you decided to accept him into your heart. I may not know what you have been through to get to Jesus, I'm sure the journey you've taken to get here was not an easy one. Be rest assured! *The old is gone!*

Look at how wonderful your life is now that you get to walk as a Son or Daughter of God! You no longer live your life with *guilt, shame* or *condemnation*! Jesus has set you free!

Every pain that you once held in your heart, pain from trauma as a child or the pain from losing a loved one, whatever pain or sorrow that lingers, give *all* of it to Jesus and he will comfort you! This life you have just entered is full of *supernatural favor* and *blessings*! Christianity is NOT boring!

I encourage you to throw away all the things that were forced on you about Christianity and move forward finding the TRUTH about Jesus Christ *first hand*! Your relationship with Jesus is personal and completely unique. No one knows Jesus like you do, and no one knows you like Jesus.

Jesus walked on water! Jesus healed the sick and raised the dead! All of these things are now yours! Some people might try and convince you that all these miracles were only for the biblical days. They will try and tell you that "miracles are no longer active in our time."

But Jesus said, *" Verily, verily, I say unto you, He that believeth on me, the works that I do shall he do also; and greater works than these shall he do; because I go unto my Father.*

John 14:12-14.KJV

If you believe in Jesus then you will be able to serve him and do the things that he did. He will be able to do greater things through you because he is with the father.

You need to take a stand now at the beginning of your journey. Will you believe the bible? Or will you believe other Christians? Will you believe in the *full* word of GOD? Or will you take out of it what you want and leave the rest?

The Bible is alive and active. If you have faith in Jesus Christ then the future of supernatural life is yours. How do we know this to be true?

"Jesus Christ is the same yesterday, and today, and forever."
Hebrews 13:8KJV

✟ Don't Let Your Fire Burn Out ✟

   The greatest part about being born again is you are now on fire for Jesus! Every part of your past life has now been washed clean! That means you are completely set free! But be careful. You must be warned. So many people experience what you're going through right now and end up letting their fire burn out.

   The unfortunate truth is that it is often other Christians who put the fire out for new Christians. They tell you things like "You need to calm down or you might burn it all up." or "I'm glad to see you're happy about Jesus, but that will go away, so be prepared."

   You will never find any place in the Bible where the Lord tells his children that they need to put down their joy of salvation!
In fact, he tells us quite the opposite.

But the fruit of the Spirit is love, joy, peace, longsuffering, gentleness, goodness, faith, Meekness, temperance: against such there is no law.
Galatians 5:22-23 KJV

How can someone take away your new-found fire for Jesus if his Spirit makes you feel *Joy*? How can anyone steal your happiness if Jesus gives you *Peace?* Some Christians will tell you to calm down because of their own experience.

They felt the same burning for Christ as you at one point. But what they failed to do is keep themselves in Jesus Christ and keep Jesus Christ in themselves! Like Jesus said*" I am the vine, ye are the branches: He that abideth in me, and I in him, the same bringeth forth much fruit: for without me ye can do nothing. John15:5 KJV*

Do not be influenced by those who have fallen back into the ways of this world. Instead of keeping the faith and holding onto their happiness in Jesus, they have attached themselves to the happiness of the world. If you want to keep the FIRE you have for Jesus, then you MUST keep your mind in the bible. *You must read the word of God daily.* If you do this, Jesus will keep your fire alive and growing!

> *For our God is a consuming fire.*
>
> *Hebrews 12:29KJV*

✝The Battle Of The Flesh Has Ended ✝ The Battle Of The Mind Has Just Begun

> *Do not be conformed to this world,*
> *but be transformed by the renewing of your mind.*
> *Romans 12:2 KJV*

Now that you've given your life to Jesus, everything has changed. Even the way that you think is now being completely renewed. If you want to begin to understand the true Love of God, then you're going to need a mind that does not hinder itself from believing in miracles. God is renewing your thoughts from the ways of the *world* to the ways of *heaven*. Jesus Christ transforms your mind by revealing to you the truth of who he is. Only His truth can renew your mind and give you a new Love for God! Glory to God!

In the past, you may have tried to read the Bible but it just didn't make sense to you. With your renewed mind, not only will the Bible become easier to read, but you will be able to immerse yourself in the word.

> *For **the word of God** is **living** and **active**.*
> *Hebrews 4:12*

As soon as Jesus began to change you by renewing your mind, the word of God went from being just ink and paper to *life* and *truth*!

> *For we wrestle not against **flesh** and **blood**, but against principalities, against powers, against the rulers of the darkness of this world, against spiritual wickedness in high places.*
>
> *Ephesians 6:12 KJV*

Your battle now as a Christian is no longer with the world, but it's with the spiritual evil *of* the world. Without a renewed mind in Christ, the battle in your mind can easily be lost!

Your old thoughts will try to keep their home in your head. Your mind has become a battlefield. It is now a fight between the *new* you in Christ and your old self. But Jesus told us not to be afraid! The weapon we use is *the word of God!*

" For the word of God is quick, and powerful, and sharper than any twoedged sword, piercing even to the dividing asunder of soul and spirit, and of the joints and marrow"
Hebrews 4:12 KJV

If negative thoughts try to enter your mind, if your old way of thinking tries to dominate your new way of thinking, or if you are about to commit sin, it's time to fight! How do you fight? You speak the word of God. You recite the word of God in your mind. You use his word to fight your battles for you.

The Lord shall fight for you, and ye shall hold your peace.
Exodus 14:14 KJV

What is the proof that you are winning the battles in your mind? There is one way I have learned to recognize that you are winning the battle in your mind. And that way is, *your thoughts fall short before they can reach your heart.* The bible says *"bringing into captivity **every thought** to the **obedience of Christ**." 2 Corinthians 10:5-6 KJV.* You are winning the battles in your mind when you take them captive in Christ before they can make an impact in your life!

With every battle won you will experience joy and peace, knowing that you are becoming more and more like Jesus! From now on, when you sin, your mind will be prepared to go to battle. Don't worry, Jesus forgave all your past sins, your present sins, and your future sins. THE BATTLE HAS ALREADY BEEN WON!

✝ Get To Know The New You ✝

Now that you're born again you're not going to be able to recognize who you are. When you accepted Jesus into your heart he instantly was given the ability to transform you from the inside out. That means there are some thoughts, wants, and desires that are leftover in the crevices of your mind that need to be removed!

After I became born again my attitude on life and the things of this world had changed. I started to let Joy and Peace rule my life instead of hatred and doubt. I begin to walk in a lifestyle of happiness that I had never experienced before in my life. When the supernatural power of God begins to uplift you and make you joyful you'll notice everything about your old self becomes boring and fruitless!

As God became more and more real in my life, everything that I used to take pleasure in became more and more *disgusting*. Everything that seemed to be what the world had to offer was revealing itself to be pointless and sinful. I could no longer tell who I was, and I liked it. Because of that, I could see that I was being freed from everything that used to cause me to sin. How did I recognize that I was becoming someone new?

Example:

Before I was born again I had a list of movies that were my all-time favorite movies. One of these movies was my favorite because it gave me feelings I used to latch on to, like the hope of falling in love or traveling the world.

One day I sat down to watch this movie. I didn't get halfway through without realizing everything about this movie was *disgusting*! Scenes that I used to enjoy were now making me sick! The cursing that used to not affect me now made me uncomfortable! The things that would excite me BEFORE I became born again now only made me feel EMPTY.

Needless to say, I stopped watching those movies. I became filled with a God who *Loves*. A God who declares victory and always promises a great outcome. So now *those* are the types of movies I enjoy watching. Movies that give you hope in a loving God who saves. I *refuse* to watch anything that would displease God. The devil uses the things of this world to give you a false hope. But when Jesus enters your life, everything the devil uses to entice the world no longer works on you.

Overcome evil with good.
Romans 12:21 KJV

I encourage you to embrace joy as you become a new you. Let your newfound joy in Christ take over the evil you were once controlled by. Rest assured that God is molding you into something new! Something you won't even recognize anymore! If the God of the universe is transforming you into a new creation, then you can be happy knowing that you are about to walk in a life that is joy everlasting.

✟ The World Strives For Happiness ✟ When God Offers Joy

I soon learned that relationship with Jesus Christ was far more joyous than watching a movie that fills you with temporary happiness. The Bible tells us that Jesus was anointed with the oil of Joy. *Hebrews 1:9*. He was the most joyful man in the world!

The Bible explains Joy as being far greater than happiness. God greatly desires for you to be happy. But it's happiness that stems from joy in Jesus that God desires for you most. Before you were born again you hungered for what the world could offer. "I just want to be happy". The world can make you happy for the wrong reasons.

Before I was born again I would get happy when others would fail in areas that I would succeed in. I would become happy when I had drinks with friends, or when I would joke about inappropriate things.

What God offers you is far more valuable. Happiness is temporary. But Joy lasts forever. Trials and temptations will still come your way. But unlike the rest of the world, we get to walk forward in Joy knowing that *eternal life* is ours.

Everything Jesus offers us is true. One thing Jesus offers us is *life ABUNDANTLY. John 10:10.* The happiness you once searched for does not compare to the constant Joy you have inherited in Jesus Christ. Joy is given to us by our FAITH. And our FAITH comes from hearing the word of GOD! Let's read some verses from the bible that will feed your JOY!

"Blessed is the man that trusteth in the Lord, and whose hope the Lord is.For he shall be as a tree planted by the waters, and that spreadeth out her roots by the river, and shall not see when heat cometh, but her leaf shall be green; and shall not be

careful in the year of drought, neither shall cease from yielding fruit"

Jerimiah 17:7-8 KJV

✝

"For I know the thoughts that I think toward you, saith the Lord, thoughts of peace, and not of evil, to give you an expected end."

Jerimiah 29:11 KJV

✝

" But my God shall supply all your need according to his riches in glory by Christ Jesus."

Phillippians 4:19 KJV

✝

"the joy of the Lord is your strength."

Nehemiah 8:10 KJV

How beautiful that the joy of the Lord is your strength!

✝ You Are Now Being Refined ✝ And Purified

For thou, O God, hast proved us: thou hast tried us, as silver is tried.
Psalms 66:10 KJV

Every time someone becomes born again (or rededicates their life) the Lord begins a process like refining Silver or Gold. The fire of the Lord comes upon you and burns up every part of you that does not look like his son Jesus. The end product always leaves only what is *pure* and *righteous*.

Are you ready? You've made the commitment. You've given your life to Jesus. Now your powerful decision to follow Christ has become Christ's Powerful decision to change you from the inside out. This process will test you to your very bones.

As God began to purify me in my life I began to look at myself in a new light. The old things that used to excite me no longer had a hold on me. So I became entirely available for whatever God had in store for me. I began to have energy that I never experienced before.

The desires of my old life were no longer relevant. But the new desires that came surprised me. As I began to draw closer to God and he began to draw closer to me, I was given a revelation on my new body and my health. Even my eating habits changed to the point where I lost 30 pounds!

Example:

The Lord spoke to me one day while I was driving to a grocery store and he began to point out all the birds in the air. And then he showed me in a vision all the animals in the mountains. There was deer running. I saw squirrels jumping from tree to tree. Then the Lord spoke and told me, "Look at all these animals. Each one is doing exactly what I have designed them to do. The deer run and they don't become weary. The Bears eat and prepare for hibernation without worrying about the coming winter. I have given these animals all the energy they need to prosper in *everything* they do."

And as I meditated on what he was showing, I heard him speak this to my heart.

"If you want to be fit for the kingdom, you need to be fit for the kingdom".

In other words, if I want to be fit for the call he's placed on my life, then I'm going to need to get fit in my body so I can have the energy to run where he tells me to run. When God tells you to run, he means RUN! My transformation was activated! The fire of God was purifying me from the inside out.

✝ Do Not Fight Your Free Gift ✝ Of Salvation

God is going to begin removing things from you that you don't want to get rid of just yet. Becoming born-again will transform your life but the fact is you still have free will. You will always run into someone who is a born-again Christian who might not have let God remove everything from them when they first became born-again. Keep in mind if you judge your walk with Jesus by the lives of others you will have trouble from the start.

I encourage you to listen to the Holy Spirit when you are being transformed! You heard God's call to come near to him. If you heard his call once, you will always hear his call. So do not question when he begins to call you to give up the things that displease him.

Example:

I used to play videogames all the time. My life was going to work and playing video games. After I became born-again God began to convict me. I enjoyed spending time with God. But my time with God was getting interrupted by my Xbox. God is a jealous God.

God is not jealous like you and I would be jealous. God is jealous when we replace the things he desires to reveal to us with things of the world. So as God was calling me to come closer to him I was obeying him, but at the same time, I was giving my energy to the things of the world. I'm not saying videogames are a sin, but I am saying that anything you put as a priority in your life ahead of God, is a sin.

God gave me the wisdom to discipline myself with video games. I had to make sacrifices to push video games away from me so I could have time with God. It did not take long at all for me to realize that my true joy is spending time with Jesus! When you seek God he begins to uplift you with his presence. It doesn't matter what the world offers to make you happy, the presence of God is joy everlasting.

It got to a point where I didn't want to play video games anymore. So I moved out in an act of faith. I put my Xbox on Craigslist and I made a decision. I was going to step away from video games until I reached maturity. Maybe one day I would be capable of playing video games again. But if that day ever came, I know that I would not let it consume my life as it did before. A week later, I sold it. I could feel the grace of God in my life.

   God wasn't disappointed in me for playing video games. But now that I accepted Jesus into my heart he was able to show me new things that would take our relationship to higher levels! How could I expect God to change my everything if I don't give him my everything! If I would have fought against him and kept my Xbox he would still love me. He would still show me new things and teach me new things. But it was because I sacrificed something that I thought was dear to me that he revealed to me what true intimacy looked like in a relationship with him.

   I don't want to miss out on my time with God. Even as you are reading this it might seem hard for you to understand that it is possible to be excited to be alone with God. If you ever want to reach that level of intimacy, then you will need to ask yourself, *what is in my life that's taking up my time with the Lord?* Don't be afraid to let him transform you. The change that's happening in you is crucial! You are being prepared to be transformed again and again for the rest of your life!

✟Prepare To Be Transformed From✟ Glory To Glory

But we all, with open face beholding as in a glass the glory of the Lord, are changed into the same image from glory to glory, even as by the Spirit of the Lord.

2 Corinthians 3:18 KJV

Accepting Christ is not the end. In fact, it's the beginning. Now that you are justified by faith, you have the ability to be transformed from Glory to Glory! That means the more you seek him the more he will reveal himself to you. It's his greatest desire to see you growing every day because *he wants you to constantly be transformed!* Look at this verse below.

It is the glory of God to conceal a thing: but the honour of kings is to search out a matter.

Proverbs 25:2 KJV

God conceals things from his children because he loves us! He loves to reveal new things to us when we show him our love and obedience for him. Jesus died so you could inherit *eternal life*. That alone is the greatest gift we could ever receive and it's free!

Yet God always wants us to go to the *next level.* Many Christians think that after your born-again the race is over. You need to understand that your life has only just begun.

Now that you have full access to God it's time you start finding out the things he has hidden for you. God has destined you for a purpose that you and only you can walk out. The only way you're going to reach new levels of understanding is if you seek out the hidden things God desires to reveal to you. How do you become changed from glory to glory? How do you search out God's concealed secrets?

Example:

When I became born-again, God started to speak to my heart. Your walk with God began because at one point he spoke to your heart. That means from now on *if* you continue to walk with God, your ability to hear his voice will only grow. (I can't tell you that enough.) Soon you will be able to hear him speak and you will be able to make decisions based on his wisdom for your life.

As God began to speak to my heart, one of the things he told me was that I was going to begin having prophetic dreams. Dreams that would have hidden meanings. Hidden secrets that I would have the pleasure to seek out. Dreams that would tell me the future. To warn me, or to give me instructions to give to someone else. (These gifts are for you also. You will read about this more in another chapter.)

After God placed this on my heart, I began to research dreams and seek God about this more and more. Until one night, sleeping in my parents basement, I had a dream. I dreamt I was walking in my basement past my workout equipment, and as I went into my bedroom there was a wine glass sitting on my desk. Only inside the wine glass was not wine, it was refried beans!

As I looked closer, the wine glass spilled over on its own and spilled the beans all over my desk. As I woke up I wrote the dream down. Writing down my dream showed God that I cherished the dreams he gives me and I will steward any dreams God shows me in the future. *Any gift God gives you needs to be cherished. If you don't cherish it and use it, God is not likely to give you more gifts.*

I went to work that day thinking about what that dream could have meant. Was I going to spill the beans on someone at work? My interpretation of the dream was useless! I gave up pondering the dream and I went on with my day. To be honest, I completely forgot about the dream.

When I got home I fell into my usual routine. I would work out, shower, then sit alone with Jesus and *sometimes* take communion. (Communion is partaking in the Lord's supper, eating the bread and drinking the wine in remembrance of Jesus's death on the cross).

This day I decided I was going to take communion. I took my cup with a little bit of wine and I took my cracker and I sat alone with God. I thanked Jesus for dying on the cross for me and I asked him to give me more wisdom and understanding. After I prayed I reached for the cup of wine and I knocked it over spilling wine all over the carpet! Wine and your moms' carpet do not mix! I ran upstairs hoping to grab a towel and some carpet cleaner. But the moment I got to the kitchen I smelled something. It was refried beans! Just like the ones I saw in my dream! My mom was making tacos! Jesus loves tacos!

My dream came flooding back to me! I remember passing my workout equipment and seeing the wine glass on my desk in my room. The exact same refried beans that were in the wine glass were in my kitchen! My mom never told me we were having tacos that day. She never told me the day before either. Only God would've known that the wine glass was going to spill, and tacos were in my near future! God bless tacos.

That night I prayed and I asked God why he showed me that? Why was it such a mystery for me to understand? God began to speak to my heart. I began to understand why dreams are so complex. I began to understand why some dreams are very strange.

God wants us to constantly seek him and ask him questions that will bring us closer to him. He wants you to seek him to find out the meaning. That dream wasn't extremely prophetic. That dream wasn't like the intense dreams you read about in the Bible. God just wanted me to know that he's with me at all times. He wanted me to know that he's with me while I pray and take communion. He wanted me to know that he's with me while I eat tacos!

That night God showed me that if I obey him and seek him he will reveal to me all kinds of secrets. He showed me how he desires to transform us from Glory to Glory. From heavenly gift to heavenly gift. It all starts by becoming a new creation in Christ!

-Chapter 2-
✝ Baptized In The Holy Spirit ✝

"In whom ye also trusted, after that ye heard the word of truth, the gospel of your salvation: in whom also after that ye believed, ye were sealed with that holy Spirit of promise"
Ephesians 1:13 KJV

Jesus is now seated at the right hand of the father. Before Jesus ascended into heaven he assured us that he would send us a helper. This helper sat with God at the beginning of time just like Jesus did. This helper would not only follow you and reveal to you all the things of God, *but this helper would live inside of you!*

In the days of Jesus, in Jerusalem, the Jews had a holy temple. Inside the Temple, behind a veil, was the presence of God. Jesus told the Pharisees "Destroy this temple and in three days I will raise it up again." John 2:19. The Pharisees didn't understand that Jesus was talking about himself. On the day Jesus died, the veil was torn from top to bottom, revealing to the jews that God's presence was no longer in a temple made by man. Three days later Jesus rose from the dead and God's presence now resides in *you*!

Know ye not that ye are the temple of God, and that the Spirit of God dwelleth in you?
1 Corinthians 3:16 KJV

Our helper is the *Holy Spirit!* The Holy Spirit living inside of you is the presence of God! *"The Spirit of truth that proceeds from the father" John 16:26 KJV.* God no longer lives in a temple made by man but lives inside of those who believe in his son Jesus Christ.
That's you! After you become born again the Holy Spirit resides *inside* of you. You do not need a special ritual to be confirmed that you have the Holy Spirit. Keep in mind, to have the Holy Spirit inside of you and to be baptized in the Holy Spirit are two different things.

✝ Speaking In Unknown Tongues ✝

When the Disciples were baptized in the Holy Spirit the bible says they spoke in tongues *"And they were all filled with the Holy Spirit and began to speak in other tongues as the Spirit gave them utterance."Acts 2:4.*

Praying in tongues is a sure sign that you have been baptized in the Holy Spirit. Some Christians will tell you that praying in tongues is not of God. All it takes is a small amount of research and you will find that tongues *are* a gift from God.

Praying in tongues is a true gift due to the power it releases, and the effect it has on your spirit. *"He that speaketh in an unknown tongue edifieth himself" 1 Corinthians 14:4 KJV.* When you pray in tongues you are not aware of what you are saying. It is a language that only God knows. Praying in tongues not only edifies your spirit but it also builds up the church!

You could be praying about a family member or a friend when you pray in tongues! But you do not know it! When you speak in tongues you are speaking in a heavenly language. When you are burdened, or in need of peace, praying in tongues will uplift you.

How do you pray in tongues? SEEK GOD! *"For he that cometh to God must believe that he is, and that he is a rewarder of them that diligently seek him." Hebrews 11:6 KJV.* God wants you to be baptized in the Holy Spirit more than you do! If you are born again and have accepted Jesus Christ into your heart, then the gift of the Holy Spirit is yours. If you want God to *activate* the gift of praying in tongues in your life then *"Ask, and it shall be given you; seek, and ye shall find; knock, and it shall be opened unto you:" Matthew 7:7 KJV*

The Holy Spirit is moving and speaking to you about *all* the things of God. The Holy Spirit is many things. Here are just a couple things the bible tells about the Holy Spirit.

✝ The Holy Spirit Is Teacher ✝

But the Comforter, which is the Holy Ghost, whom the Father will send in my name, he shall teach you all things, and bring all things to your remembrance, whatsoever I have said unto you.
John 14:26 KJV

We are meant to live this life by the word of the LORD *and* by the Holy Spirit. It would be a scary world if you relied on all of your understanding of the Bible to come from a human teacher! We have some powerful men and women of God that teach the gospel of Jesus Christ all around the world. The same Holy Spirit that lives in them now lives in you! You do not need the world to teach you what you should do or how you should believe. *THE HOLY SPIRIT IS YOUR TEACHER!*

But the anointing which ye have received of him abideth in you, and ye need not that any man teach you: but as the same anointing teacheth you of all things, and is truth, and is no lie, and even as it hath taught you, ye shall abide in him.

1 John 2:27 KJV

The Scripture can be confusing to many unbelievers. The bible tells us that *"the minds of unbelievers are closed".* 2 Corinthians 3:14 KJV. Only Jesus can give an understanding of the word of God through the Holy Spirit. When you received the Holy Spirit the Bible became living and active in your life. Because of the Holy Spirit, you get to read what God says as if he said it directly to you. Without the Holy Spirit, your new life in Christ would not be possible.

A teacher is only as good as the student listens. In order for the Holy Spirit to teach you, you're going to need to dedicate yourself to listening. It took faith for you to hear God and become born again.

"Faith comes by hearing, and hearing by the word of God" Romans 10:17KJV. God loves it when his children listen to the Holy Spirit and obey. The best way to develop your intimacy with the Holy Spirit is to take notes.

The more you desire to prosper in your education, the more your life will be blessed in the presence of God. As you begin to read the Bible you must allow the Holy Spirit to guide you and speak to you about all the mysteries of the word of God. Take heed what you hear. *With the same measure you use, it will be measured to you; and to you who hear, more will be given. Mark 4:24KJV*

The Bible is not a book written by a man. *"All scripture is given by inspiration of God, and is profitable for doctrine, for reproof, for correction, for instruction in righteousness" 2 Timothy 3:16 KJV*. So don't be afraid to take notes and write in your Bible. Don't be afraid to highlight verses that the Holy Spirit stirs up in your heart. You're going to have a lot of bibles in your lifetime. The more torn your Bible is, the less torn your Spirit will be.

With the Holy Spirit as your only teacher, you will never have to worry about being deceived. No one will be able to try and convince you of anything that is not of God. The Holy Spirit will remind you of specific verses in the Bible that will be able to shut down anything the devil tries to throw at you. Become confident in letting the Holy Spirit guide you and teach you! Then you will be able to recognize other Christians and teach one another in the wisdom and revelation you have received from the Holy Spirit.

Let the word of Christ dwell in you richly in all wisdom; teaching and admonishing one another

Colossians 3:16 KJV

✝ The Holy Spirit Is Comforter ✝

Your new life as a Christian does not mean you will avoid trials. But it does mean that you will no longer be alone in your trials! God has been watching over you since the day he began creating you in your mother's womb.

In fact, the Bible says that *"Before I formed thee in the belly I knew thee" Jeremiah 1:5 KJV*. The difference between the *old* you and the *new* you is the Wisdom and Power of the Holy Spirit living *inside* of you!

The Holy Spirit promises to comfort you in any situation life can throw at you. When chaos enters your life or when negative thoughts come, the Holy Spirit will remind you of God's word.

For I know the plans I have for you," declares the LORD, "plans to prosper you and not to harm you, plans to give you hope and a future.

Jeremiah 29:11

Fear thou not; for I am with thee: be not dismayed; for I am thy God: I will strengthen thee; yea, I will help thee; yea, I will uphold thee with the right hand of my righteousness.
Isaiah 41:10 KJV

Nothing you go through will ever overtake you! Nothing this life puts in your path will cause you to fall! Now that you have the Holy Spirit you will walk in the *light* of life. You will be aware of the *Blessings* of the LORD and God's *Favor* in your walk with Him. All of this will be yours for the GLORY OF THE LORD GOD! AMEN!

✝ Do Not Grieve The Holy Spirit ✝

- *Eternal life*
- *Power over all forms of darkness*
- *Love from the father*

These are just some of the things you get to delight yourself in as a new believer in Christ. Do not take advantage of the blessings of God and use them as an excuse to sin, therefore grieving the Holy Spirit.

The Holy Spirit is sensitive to the things of God and will never partake in the wicked things of the world. When you grieve the Holy Spirit you push away the comfort that you have been blessed with. Grieving the Holy Spirit can look like giving the guy that cut you off on the road half a peace sign. You grieve the Spirit when you think sexual thoughts about a woman you see when you're out shopping. Or when you choose not to help someone when you clearly had the opportunity to help.

Keep your peace Brothers and Sisters. If you grieve the Holy Spirit, repent and all things will be made new. We all grieve the Holy Spirit in our lives. It's what we do after that is the true test.

*And grieve not the Holy Spirit of God, whereby ye are sealed unto the day of redemption. Let all **bitterness** and **wrath** and **anger** and **clamor** and **evil speaking** be put away from you, with all **malice**; and be ye **kind** one to another, **tenderhearted**, **forgiving** one another, even as God for Christ's sake hath forgiven you.*

Ephesians 4:30-32.KJV

The Holy Spirit is called many things. Every time you think you understand the Holy Spirit, you get a new revelation of the knowledge and power of the Spirit. If you want the Holy Spirit to move in your life and teach you new things daily, you need to be still. Keep your mind clean. Repent of your sins immediately and let Jesus wash you daily. The Holy Spirit is your best friend. He will never let you down.

-Chapter 3-
✝ The Supernatural ✝
Is Your Reality

And it shall come to pass in the last days, saith God, I will pour out of my Spirit upon all flesh: and your sons and your daughters shall prophesy, and your young men shall see visions, and your old men shall dream dreams:
Acts 2:17 KJV

You now get to embrace the supernatural world around you! The world embraces evil every day on TV and music. Much of the church believes that demons are running rampant. Yet they don't believe that angels are moving even more so! If you believe that evil has power over people's lives, then you better believe that Jesus has *all* power over your life.

The word of God is truth. That means everything in the bible is true. Jesus walked on water. Jesus cast out devils. *All* the supernatural things Jesus did are now for *you*. If you have any trouble believing that you can do all the things of Christ, then you need to remember exactly what God did to bring you to Jesus. He moved into your heart and changed you forever. You believe without a doubt that God exists and he brought his son Jesus back from the dead. But it's hard for you to believe that you can cast out demons? It's hard to believe that ministering angels help you in your day to day life?

Your new supernatural life was given to you by your inheritance in Jesus Christ! *"In whom also we have obtained an inheritance," Ephesians 1:11 KJV.* The kingdom is now yours! You are an heir of the kingdom! *"Wherefore thou art no more a servant, but a son; and if a son, then an heir of God through Christ." Galatians 4:7 KJV.* If you are a Son or Daughter of God then you get to receive all that the Father has as your inheritance. Everything in your father's house is yours!

I am so excited to teach you some of the supernatural things that God has destined for you to walk in. The unseen realm is about to become more real to you than you could ever imagine. The veil between this world and the heavenly realm is thinner than ever. But because it is real, and because you can access it, you need to be aware of the responsibility of a supernatural life.

✝ You Must Be Warned ✝

"For unto whomsoever much is given, of him shall be much required" Luke 12:48 KJV

If you want to be trusted with the gifts of the supernatural you must first keep God above everything. Many Christians have become more interested in the supernatural things of God and neglected their relationship *with* God. When God can trust you to walk in the supernatural without losing your intimacy with his son Jesus, *then* he will begin to reveal to you the wonders of heaven.

God has been watching over you and taking care of you all your life. He does not need to show you his angels to reveal his love for you. If you want to have dreams that show you the future, if you desire to get words of knowledge about people you have never met before, you must first walk in maturity to the obedience of Christ. The first sign of maturity is someone who admits to their mistakes. Anyone who is a mature man or woman of God is constantly obedient to the will of God.

Would you give the keys to your car to your five-year-old Son or Daughter? Would you feed your brand new baby a T-Bone steak? A child does not get anything from their Father until they are mature and can be fully trusted. A child does not inherit the possessions of their Father until they reach maturity. Your Father in heaven desires to give you everything that is His. You are his child and he loves you!

If you want to partake in the supernatural things of God, you need to abide in Jesus Christ. The only requirement is to Love Jesus with all your heart and with all your mind. You must hunger for Jesus above everything else. You must be willing to sacrifice anything for Jesus when he calls your name.

God will show you all the manifestations of heaven. God will teach you how to walk in the realm of the supernatural. It is only when you are ready will he reveal to you the miracles and wonders of heaven. Do you want to see angels? Do you want to have visions and dreams? How hungry are you for Jesus? How much are you willing to sacrifice to be intimately connected to God?

Let's dive into what God has in store for you now that you are born-again. Just remember. God only reveals himself to those who love him with all of their heart.

You will seek me and find me when you seek me with all your heart.
Jeremiah 29:13 KJV

✞ Heavenly Visions ✞

I the Lord will make myself known unto him in a vision, and will speak unto him in a dream.
Numbers 12:6 KJV

Visions are an important part of your intimacy with God. What is a vision? A vision is a divine appearance granted by God to grow his kingdom. God can take you to heaven in a vision. He can show you things that can happen in the future that would change someone's life forever. Whatever God believes is important enough to reveal to you will be given to you in a vision.

Visions can happen at any time of the day or night. Oftentimes a vision can be like having a heavy daydream. My first vision was in a dream. I became instantly aware that I was in a vision.

Everything became as real in the dream as life is in the natural. In the Vision, I was caught up into heaven and was given a very intimate message from God.

Visions can confirm things that God has placed on your heart since you were a child. Visions can give you instructions on how to handle a specific situation. Some visions can give you insight into what will happen in the future. Many times throughout the Bible the LORD gave a vision to someone who needed to be instructed to lead a great move of God.

Whatever the vision God may give you, God is trusting you to seek him about what you may have seen and experienced. Sometimes a vision can be like dreams and you might need to seek God for the full interpretation of the vision. Every vision from God will move you closer to him and the knowledge of who he is.

Keep Jesus as the most important person in your life. Never compromise your relationship with him because of visions. If you hold fast to your love in Christ, he will continue to give you visions that will grow the Kingdom and bring people closer to God!

Example:

   In 2019 I attended a conference hosted by Todd White called Power And Love. On the first day of this conference, I sat at the back of the church listening to the message when a man came and sat in front of me. As he sat down I found myself asking God to give me a word for him.

   As soon as I asked God, I was instantly placed in a vision. I saw this man as a young child. As this man was growing up I watched as some terrible things were done to him. Things that no young boy should ever go through. As I continued to watch him grow older in this vision, I saw that he had hardness in his heart towards God for the things that had happened to him.

   As I watched him grow up into the man he was now, I saw in a vision a large clay pot floating above his head. Water was flowing from heaven into this clay pot and was hitting the bottom. Then I hear the LORD speak. "I desire to pour out my Spirit on this man. He has hindered me from reaching him by the hardness of his heart. Tell him that I desire to be a greater father to him than his earthly father ever was, then, I will break through the bottom of this clay jar and flow over him with water everlasting" This was a heavy vision that made me joyful that God would use me to speak to this man.

Just as the vision was over, the speaker told us to break off into groups and ask God to reveal things to us about each other that only God would know. How crazy is that! It was *God* that wanted to say something to this man, not me!

As we stood up I tapped on his shoulder and I told him "My friend, God has something big to tell you" I watched him as I began to tell him all that God had shown me since he first sat down. I watched his face as piece by piece he began to break down. Everything that God had shown me was true. He was hardened in his heart from what had happened to him as a child. He had distanced himself from God because of the lack of a loving father.

I told him exactly what God had told me to say. He began to break down as I told him that God wanted to be his true father now. This was a great moment. He came to this conference because of his wife. He told me that even she did not know of the things that had happened to him.

I told him that if he gave the pain of the past to God, then God would break through the bottom of his broken spirit and pour out on him Comfort and Joy that can only be given by a loving father. Before I left I prophesied over him and told him "If you receive God this day, you will be an entirely new man by the end of this conference"

As I hugged him goodbye I began to cry. I am not a special Christian. My mom was not given a visitation from an angel the night I was born and told that she was going to give birth to a prophet. I am just like you. I seek God for the greater things. I desire to be used for the glory of God. This man was radically changed that day and I had nothing to do with it.

Visions are for you. It's important we thank God for every vision. It is more important that we do not find our identity in visions. We are sons and daughters of God. We have the grace of God to receive visions for the sole purpose of glorifying God and God alone. If we humble ourselves, it will be God's pleasure to give us visions and dreams that will glorify Him and bring us into deeper intimacy with Jesus Christ.

✞ Heavenly Dreams ✞

I am a dreamer. God spoke to me in 2016 and showed me that I will now have prophetic dreams. Ever since that night, I have had a dream or a vision. Every night. When God gives you a gift, he makes sure you receive it and keep it.

If it wasn't for dreams Jesus would have died as a child! Without dreams, an angel would never have told Joseph to take Mary and Jesus to Egypt before Herod could kill him. It was because of dreams that Joseph (the son of Jacob) found favor with Pharo and saved the Hebrews.

God wants to give you dreams that will open your eyes to his never-ending love. Every God-given dream is an opportunity to get to know God in a new way. He will show you things that will cause you to be amazed at his constant presence in your life.

Example:
The "I Am With You" Dreams

Not every dream will be an explosion of prophetic destiny. In fact, most times God will give you a

dream that will simply remind you of his love. In 2018 I had a dream. In that dream, I woke up and looked in the mirror to find that I had shaved my face. At that time I was growing out my beard so I was surprised to see a shaved face!
Only my face in the dream was different. I still had a little bit of scruff but what shocked me was my jawline was not my own! My face had some bald spots that I had never had before. Patches of hair were missing! Needless to say, I was freaking out.

   After I woke up I remember frantically feeling my chin to make sure my beard was still on my face. I thought I had sleepwalked into my bathroom and shaved! I was relieved to find that my poor attempt at a beard was still attached. Later that day I had a dinner meeting with some family friends. Much like a lot of the time, I had written the dream down, then completely forgotten about it.

   As I arrived at the restaurant I greeted everyone and was seated next to an old friend. He looked at the waitress to tell her his order and I was instantly shocked! His face, his jawline, the patches of hair missing, it was exactly what I had seen the night before in my dream! Every detail, to the way he spoke and moved his head, to the shape his jaw made when he spoke! Every detail of his face was exactly what I had on my face in the dream!

I hadn't spoken to this friend in a long time. I had no idea he could even grow a beard! (Or lack thereof). I was so surprised, but what could I do? Say "hey man I had your face last night". What?

What did this mean? I thought to myself, do I need to pray for him? Should I pray God fills in the bald spots and gives him a Duck Dynasty beard? WHAT DO I DO GOD?!

After I began to calm down I heard God speak to my heart.
"I will be with you always James."

God just wanted me to know that I was in the exact spot he wanted me to be. He used a friend to show me that I was following the path he had put me on. When you obey the will of God and walk in purity, God will assure you in dreams that you are exactly where he planned for you to be. It is so wonderful to get little gems from God every day! Every day you can have prophetic moves of God that simply tell you "I'm with you today my child."

You may have had a dream of a building you have never seen before or a dream of an old friend you haven't talked to in a while. Then the next day you see the building! You run into your old friend! God wants you to seek him every day! If you love him well, it will be his pleasure to show you the work of his hands in your life. God knows what you are going to do tomorrow. He knows who you will be with. It doesn't matter where you are or what you are doing, he is with you.

Example: The Prophetic Dreams

God desires to constantly give you new revelation. (New understanding of his will pertaining to your life and your calling). Some God-given dreams will impact your life *forever*. You will learn that many of the things God reveals to you must remain a secret between you and God.

When you keep the secrets of God, you show him that you desire intimacy with him more than anything in the world. It is so beautiful that the God of the universe will teach you secrets that are only between *you* and *him*!

Some parts of this dream need to be kept a secret. I am excited to tell you about the parts he will allow me to reveal! This dream was not only prophetic but it was exactly what I needed at that moment in my life. That's what God does. He loves to bring you everything you need in his perfect timing.

In this dream, I was standing at the top of a staircase that leads to a dark basement. I could feel the presence of evil trying to attach itself to me. I was aware that the enemy was furious at the man I was becoming. I'm sure you have had a dream of evil surrounding you. A dream where you can feel the presence of demons trying to put fear in you.

I was aware that evil was trying to attack me. I was able to run away from the basement and found myself near a church. In the church, I saw lovely people who loved Jesus. I asked many people in the church for help but they were filled with fear and did not know the word of God enough to rebuke the presence of evil from me.

After continuing to search for help I found myself with people that were a part of a Christian school that I have admired for a long time. One of the students was sensitive in the spirit and when he came close to me he could feel the presence of evil that was following me. But he couldn't do anything about it! Even he was filled with fear and didn't know how to help me!

   After I realized it was just me and this evil presence, I took the journey back to the top of the staircase that led to the dark basement. I had an internal knowing that the demons were going to come out of the basement and reveal themselves to me in their true forms. The first came out looking like a giant scorpion. As it came up the stairs I repeated: "I am a son of God". The demon became angry and tried to enter me but it failed!

   The second demon came up the stairs looking like a normal man. He was wearing a suit and tie and tried to look respectable. As he came up the stairs and tried to enter me I repeated: "Only Jesus Christ Can Live In Me". He also became angry and failed to enter me. I could tell more demons were trying to come up the stairs but I had enough! I was done! I stood boldly in front of any evil that was going to face me! I would not be moved! At that moment I woke up.

As I woke up the Holy Spirit instantly gave me the interpretation of the dream.

If God gives you a prophetic dream, the Holy Spirit will give you the interpretation.

I was about to be moved into a life of full-time Ministry! The demons were trying their best to come at me because they could see the authority of God in my life. They could see the blessings God was pouring out on me to use me to minister to the church! Demonic activity will increase when God is preparing you for a great commission.

The devil will send all his worthless demons to do everything they can to distract you from walking in the calling God has placed on your life.

The Holy Spirit revealed to me that I am now ready to walk in the anointing to teach and build up the Church. I wanted so desperately for someone to command the evil to go from me. The Holy Spirit showed me that I have authority over all the forces of darkness, but most importantly, I am now able to minister to the church on how to use the authority for themselves!

So many churches around the world are full of the Holy Spirit and are in love with Jesus, but they do not know how to use their authority to help others! In the dream, I would go from church to church asking for help but no one knew how to take power over evil.

Even the man who was a student at the Christian school couldn't help me. We are raising a generation of believers to know of the *power* of God, but we are not teaching them how to use the *authority* of God!

If you are ready to live a supernatural life you must be aware that the devil will always try to stop you from receiving the supernatural gifts of God. Nowhere in the bible did God tell you to beg Him to do something about the devil. He gave *you* the authority over *all* the forces of darkness!

✝ Words Of Knowledge ✝ And Prophecy

Many Christians confuse Prophecy for words of knowledge. When you *prophesy*, you tell someone what God put on your heart about their *future*. You may prophesy to someone about someone getting a new job. You might prophesy to someone about a coming opportunity to move to another state. Whatever God puts on your heart when you prophesy will be a future event that will occur. When you prophesy accurately God gets the glory and it often gives great faith to the one you prophesy over.

Words of knowledge are when you hear from God about something that happened to someone in their past or something they are currently going through. A word of knowledge is an important way for God to use you to show someone how much God loves them and how much he is always with them. A word of knowledge can remind someone how much God knows who they are.

Example:
✟Word Of Knowledge✟

In 2018 I was at a conference in Denver Colorado with Shawn Bolz. Shawn Bolz is a prophet who works greatly in words of knowledge. I highly recommend you get his teachings and study guides. During the conference, we were set up in groups of two and asked to seek God for a word for the other person.

I was partnered with a woman my age. Let's just call her Sarah. As I shook Sarah's hand I instantly began to get a word about her previous relationship. I asked her if she had an ex-fiance. She looked at me in shock and she began to cry.

As I looked at her I began to cry also. I saw that she had an ex-fiance and he had died in a car crash not too long ago. I saw what she has been going through and I saw that she has been feeling guilty for asking God to bring her a husband. I told her what God was showing me and she confirmed that everything was true.

I told her that God was with her the entire time. I told her that the devil comes to steal, kill, and destroy. God loved her fiance and it was not God's fault that this tragedy happened. I told her that God knows that she has been praying for a husband and she does not need to feel guilty. Her fiance would have wanted her to move on and be happy.

I want you to imagine what she was feeling. God was revealing to her the biggest tragedy that she has ever experienced. God was showing her that he has been with her and holding her the entire time. Because of a word of knowledge she was shown that God is always with her and He will return everything the devil stole from her with interest.

   This is the power of receiving a word of knowledge from the Holy Spirit. Later in the conference, Shawn Bolz said something that will stay with me forever. He said, "One word of knowledge can do more than fifty sessions with a therapist". In this brief interaction, Sarah was shown that God knows the very deepest pain that she holds. God showed her that he cares deeply for her and he will always watch over her as the loving father that He is.

   I want to encourage you to walk out and practice the gift of Word of Knowledge. Everyone who receives Jesus as LORD and savior has the ability to receive a word for someone. I must ask you, if Jesus gives you a word, will you step out? It can be nerve-wracking to walk up to a stranger and tell them that you believe God has spoken to your heart about them.

   If you don't take a step of courage then who will? If you walk away unsure if God had really spoken to you, how will you grow in this gift? Taking the first step is a sign of faith that God wants to see in his born again sons and daughters. If you believe God has spoken to your heart about someone, take a leap of faith and watch as God is glorified by your obedience.

✟ Prophecy ✟

Prophecy is an important way God speaks to his children about the future. God loves to reveal to his children that he has a beautiful life planned for them. Prophecy is a large subject that can be better understood when a new believer in Christ has time to mature. You do not need to be a prophet to prophesy. But you must be a born-again Christian who is living a pure and holy life. Keep in mind that the LORD chooses his prophets.

No man or woman should ever call themselves a prophet unless the LORD reveals it to them by a powerful visitation. Even still, a true prophet will not advertise the anointing. A word from a prophet can change the future of a Church. A word of God that is given to a prophet could save the lives of many. The responsibility of a prophet is so great that many new believers desire to prophesy but they can end up doing more bad than good.

Prophecy might seem exciting if you are a new believer but you must remember, prophecy is a blessing for mature Christians. Keeping your relationship with Jesus strong will always give you opportunities to receive a word of knowledge or to prophesy over someone.

If you truly love others then you will not take the risk of prophesying to someone until you're confident God has spoken to your heart. If you want to Prophesy, if you want to receive Words Of Knowledge, then you must *"Ask, and it shall be given you; seek, and ye shall find; knock, and it shall be opened unto you." Matthew 7:7KJV.*

-Chapter 4-
✝ Take Up Your ✝ New Authority

Behold, I give unto you power to tread on serpents and scorpions, and over all the power of the enemy: and nothing shall by any means hurt you.
Luke 10:19 KJV

You were given authority when you became born again. What kind of authority? Your authority is over the evil forces of the world. You will never fear evil again. You not only have authority to command evil forces in people but you also have authority over any evil that tries to hinder the plans God has made for you.

You must take *up your God-given authority daily.* You can change the outcome of the salvation of your loved ones. You can be the reason someone gets set free from a demon that has plagued them since childhood. You have the authority to rebuke evil from attacking your children! Keep in mind we do not command people, but we have the authority over the evil in or around people.

✝ Give The Devil A Bad Day ✝

And the God of peace shall bruise Satan under your feet
Romans 16:20 KJV

The devil hates it when you leave your house. The same spirit that raised Jesus from the dead lives in you. That means as soon as you walk into a room the devil knows you're there. The Holy Spirit announces your arrival and the devil is forced to do anything you tell him to do. Including leave.

Have you ever walked into a store and felt uneasy? Like something was wrong? If a Christian has not taken authority over a place then evil will invade. You can give the devil a bad day by announcing "Hey devil, you're not gonna harm anyone while I'm here, it's time for you to go!".

I highly recommend that you take up your authority over your home and your workplace. We do not have time to be concerned about what evil is doing around us while we go from place to place! We are called to represent Jesus. There's no better way to represent Jesus then by subduing the devil and walking in perfect peace.

Example:

Every morning my daughter and I pray. We first acknowledge that we are seated with Christ Jesus at the right hand of the father.

Hath raised us up together, and made us sit together in heavenly places in Christ Jesus
Ephesians 2:6 KJV

We thank God for all that he has given us. Then we glorify God by using our authority over all the forces of darkness. We plead the Blood of Jesus over our family, our house and our loved ones. Finally, we take our authority over her school.

Before I drop her off we hold hands and pray "In the name of Jesus we bind anyone who would try to harm any of these children. We plead the Blood of Jesus over this school *and* the land. We rebuke any evil that tries to come between the good works the LORD has ordained for these children today. We bind all evil from harming the students or the staff in Jesus' name. Amen."

The devil hates it when you open your mouth. If witches can throw a curse then we can command a blessing. The best part is, *we serve the one who* created the one that they serve. That means that the power in us will ALWAYS overcome the power of the devil.

> *Ye are of God, little children, and have overcome them: because greater is he that is in you, than he that is in the world.*
> *1 John 4:4 KJV*

✝ Supernatural Authority ✝

Heal the sick, cleanse the lepers, raise the dead, cast out devils: freely ye have received, freely give.
Matthew 10:8 KJV

Yes, you can heal the sick. Yes, you can cast out devils. *All* of these things are freely given to you by your authority in Christ. The name of Jesus is powerful. But first I want you to focus on using supernatural authority in your own life before you try to use it in someone else's. Being born-again means exactly that. You are a baby. How can you expect to heal the sick if you do not first take authority over your own body when you're sick? How do you plan on casting out devils if you do not subdue any devils that might be attacking you?

Next time you have a sore throat, remind yourself, I have authority over sickness. Then begin to speak to your sickness as if you would someone else. Place your hand where you have pain and declare that you are healed in Jesus' name. Jesus told you to heal the sick in his name. He didn't tell you to ask him to do it. Jesus Christ lives in you. If Jesus doesn't have a sore throat, then neither do you.

With his stripes we are healed
Isaiah 53:5 KJV

Experiencing the power of the name of Jesus in your own life will give you the faith to use it in others. Take authority over your house first and see how the LORD changes the atmosphere. Do the same at your workplace. You will become confident in your authority when you begin to see that demons are no longer at work when you show up. Casting out demons is a powerful way to glorify God and set the captives free. But you must have the wisdom to know when someone is being tormented by evil or if someone is just having a bad day.

I would have you raising the dead and healing the sick as soon as possible. None the less I know the importance of a small beginning. Take time to get to know Jesus. Every step towards him will build you up into his wisdom and knowledge. Surrounding yourself with his word will fill you with his authority. Read the word and build your faith.

Delight yourself in the LORD and he will establish every step you take. The best way to know how to use your authority is to learn how Jesus used his authority on the earth. All the gifts the LORD has given you will best be learned in the secret place.

-Chapter 5-
✟ Remaining In ✟
The Secret Place

"He that dwelleth in the secret place of the most High shall abide under the shadow of the Almighty."
Psalm 91:1 KJV

    This final chapter is the most important of all. All the gifts of the Spirit, the visions, dreams, and heavenly encounters are pointless if you do not remain in constant intimacy with Jesus Christ. The secret place is your personal time with Jesus. It can be a closet, an office, or even a garage. The secret place is anywhere you can get away from everyone else and pour out your heart to Jesus. In the secret place, Jesus teaches you his will and his appointed destiny for your life. The secret place is where you grow closer and closer to God.

But thou, when thou prayest, enter into thy closet, and when thou hast shut thy door, pray to thy Father which is in secret; and thy Father which seeth in secret shall reward thee openly.
Matthew 6:6 KJV

The intense love of God in your life is a result of you seeking Jesus! There's nothing you can do that will make God love you more. If you desire to move forward in your new life in Christ with exceeding joy and peace, then all you must do is dwell in intimacy with Jesus.

You are a child of God. You do not belong to this world. If you continue to please the world and take part in what the world does, then your walk with Jesus will be hindered. If you want a life of constant awareness of God's love for you then you must keep your relationship with Jesus as the most important thing. The secret place is your new classroom and the teacher is the Spirit of God.

✝ In Jesus You Will Not Be Moved ✝

Jesus spoke in parables. A parable is a story that explains spiritual understanding. One of the parables Jesus spoke was the parable of the sower.

Then he told them many things in parables, saying:"A farmer went out to sow his seed. As he was scattering the seed, some fell along the path,

and the birds came and ate it up. Some fell on rocky places, where it did not have much soil. It sprang up quickly, because the soil was shallow. But when the sun came up, the plants were scorched, and they withered because they had no root. Other seed fell among thorns, which grew up and choked the plants. Still other seed fell on **good soil***, where it produced a crop—a hundred, sixty or thirty times what was sown. Whoever has ears, let them hear."*
Matthew 13: 3-9 NIV

The seed is the word of God being placed in your mind or your "soil." Jesus Makes it clear how his word should impact your spiritual life.

"Listen then to what the parable of the sower means: When anyone hears the message about the kingdom and does not understand it, the evil one comes and snatches away what was sown in their heart. This is the seed sown along the path. The seed falling on rocky ground refers to someone who hears the word and at once receives it with joy. But since they have no root, they last only a short time. When trouble or persecution comes because of the word, they quickly fall away. The seed falling among the thorns refers to someone who hears the word, but the worries of this life and the

deceitfulness of wealth choke the word, making it unfruitful. But the seed falling on **good soil** *refers to someone who hears the word and understands it. This is the one who produces a crop, yielding a hundred, sixty or thirty times what was sown."*
Matthew 13:18-23 NIV

Receive the word of God in your heart like a seed planted in *good soil*. A seed planted in good soil will take root and produce fruit for many lifetimes. In the same way, the word planted in your heart and taking root will produce fruit that will carry your intimacy with Jesus from glory to glory. The crop of your spiritual life will multiply what was sown into your heart. Planting the word in your heart guarantees that the devil will never stand a chance at interrupting your intimate time in the secret place with the LORD.

Submit yourselves therefore to God. Resist the devil, and he will flee from you.
James 4:7 KJV

✝ Always Move Closer ✝
To Your Loving God

Draw nigh to God, and he will draw nigh to you.
James 4:8 KJV

When you take one step towards God, He takes seven steps toward you. This is the key to remaining joyful in your personal time with Jesus. Sometimes we feel like we are trying our best to come closer to God but it's not working. I assure you if you are seeking God then he is coming close to you. Perhaps he is waiting for you to make the correct move towards him. Yes, we can come close to God by reading His word, worshiping him and lifting our hands. But if we are still not feeling him come close to us then it's time we go to the secret place.

When we enter the secret place we give God access to our full spirit and mind. If you fully surrender to God he will begin to speak to you about all the things in your life that he wants to use for the kingdom. You will feel his presence and his love when you give him every part of you. Hold nothing back from God and he will hold nothing back from you.

Coming close to God is the joy of your new born-again life. God has a plan for your life that he wants to direct you into. Seeking God about everything in your life will manifest his destiny that he planned for you since before you were born.

In all your ways submit to him, and he will make your paths straight.
Proverbs 3:6 KJV

Example:

After I became born-again I began to come closer to God with my free time. I would put my kids to bed then sit alone with God. I would welcome him into every crevice of my mind. After a while I realized that he was calling me to change some things about my character. Certain things I would do in my life were unpleasing to God.

God favors obedience over sacrifice. *Behold, to obey is better than sacrifice 1 Samuel 15:22KJV.* I decided to Obey the voice of God. I was going to stop doing all the things that God was displeased with in order to be obedient to his will. So I stopped getting mad at people when I was on the road. I stopped questioning people's life decisions and I replaced my judgment with Love.

   I had to force myself to be constantly aware of how I thought about people. Every step I took to capture disobedient thoughts led me to the realization of why God was displeased with me. I was not living as if God was sitting next to me every day. I was not being kind to people in my own mind. And because of this I was hindered from letting God come close to me. Even when I was trying my best to come close to him.

   Then something changed. As I began to purify my way of thinking about people, God began to make a change in me of his own. I was noticing the presence of God in the secret place. As I came close to God, God came close to me. I began to understand that he always comes close to those who seek him. But he is not able to manifest his presence until you obey him.

   My life changed from that moment on. I cannot express to you enough the importance of the secret place. In the secret place, God will give you the battle plans for the future. He will show you the purpose of what might be happening in your life. God desires to mold you and uplift you for his glory. All that you need to sustain a life of love and abundance is to come closer to God in the secret place and God will come close to you.

✝ Hearing The Voice Of God ✝

Hearing the voice of Jesus is the most wonderful confirmation that we are his children.

My sheep hear my voice, and I know them, and they follow me:
And I give unto them eternal life; and they shall never perish, neither shall any man pluck them out of my hand.

John 27:27-28 KJV

I have always hoped that one day God would talk to me in an audible voice. I know in some instances he can and will do that. But that is not the main way God speaks to his children. It would be a sign of your immaturity if God needed to talk to you in an audible voice all the time. The bible tells us that we should be so close to God that he can guide us with his eyes. Psalms 32:8.

I have found two main ways that God will speak to us.

1. By Our Peace

2. By The Word Of God

1. By Our Peace
Example:

I used to be a worship leader in a wonderful church in Colorado. I enjoyed leading worship in the summer because I loved to ride my Harley Davidson to church. After church, I would worship God on my bike and fellowship with him on the way home. Colorado is a perfect place to worship God on two wheels.

One Sunday after church I had decided I was going to go the long way home. At a stoplight, I could feel something was wrong. My peace was gone. I suddenly was no longer excited to ride home with the LORD and speak with him. I had no idea why I felt this way. When I left the church I was filled with joy about this ride I was about to take. Why did something in me stop my joy?

Then, before the light turned green, I heard a voice in my spirit. I could feel the Holy Spirit telling me to go a different way. I looked left to the direction I was going and I felt no peace. Then when I looked right, I could feel peace. But I didn't want to go right. I was dedicated to taking a long way home. I wasn't sure why I felt that way at the time but I did everything to ignore my absence of peace.

So I went the way I wanted to go. I went Left. The ride was still beautiful. I still fellowshipped with God and let his presence fill me with joy. The only problem was I noticed something with my bike.
I was beginning to wobble! I don't know if you have ever gotten the speed wobbles while riding a thousand-pound bike, but it will humble you real quick.

I prayed "Jesus please let me come to a complete stop before my face is introduced to the pavement."

I was able to take control of the bike and come to a complete stop in the middle of the road. Praise God. I thought to myself "What is happening?" I got off the bike and sure enough, I had a flat tire. I had just put brand new tires on my bike and there it was, a nail had stopped my plans for a beautiful ride home.

I called a church buddy to come to pick me up and praise God for that. A brother in Christ is a brother for life. It wasn't until we were loading my bike onto his trailer that I remembered when I lost my peace. At that moment the Holy Spirit hit me and I heard "I told you to go right James."

Instantly I knew that God was showing me a better way. How many times have I heard the voice of God and ignored it? Where would I be today if I had listened to the Holy Spirit years ago? I understood that most of the time it's God talking to us when we lose our Peace. *Especially when we are asked to do something that we don't want to do!*

If there's something in your life that you want but you are not sure if it's God's will. I suggest you pray about it. I recommend that you sit alone with God and tell him about your plans. If you continue to ask God about it and you increase in your desire to do it, then I believe that God will support you. As long as what you want is biblical.

  But if you begin to lose your peace about anything in your life, especially after you bring it to God, then I would recommend changing your plans and moving on. Because of this experience I have learned to hear the voice of God in a whole new way. If I would have decided to keep my peace and go right, I would have made it home without any problems. But because of my inability to listen to the Holy Spirit, I was forced to pay a bunch of money to fix a brand new tire. Now I know that if my peace ever leaves me then it's time to listen to the voice of God. Your peace in the secret place will keep your mind on the voice of Jesus.

And the peace of God, which passeth all understanding, shall keep your hearts and minds through Christ Jesus.
Philippians 4:7 KJV

2. By The Word Of God

  Most of the time I hear the voice of God in my life is by reading the Bible. I believe that this is the primary way God speaks to us. All that we will ever need is written in the Bible. The answer to all of our problems and concerns is already given to us by the word of God.

I used to hope that Jesus would just speak to me and tell me that everything will be ok. But it's through life lessons that I concluded that we can always hear the voice of the LORD when we read our Bibles. God already thought of every solution to any problem you could ever face. Including the problems that have not yet revealed themselves. Everything comes back to Jesus and the gospel no matter what's going on.

I challenge you to seek the voice of God in the Bible over every situation you are in. Whether you have a need or if you just want to get to know our creator better. Our God is a loving father. He is interested in every part of your life. He deeply cares about all of your interests and concerns. Lean on God and he will sustain you. Tell him your situation and he will speak to you. The creator of the universe is in your body and he wants to speak to you more than you want to listen. Getting in the secret place is where you meet with Jesus and learn how to grow as a new believer in Christ.

Conclusion

Jesus will fill in all the blanks you may have needed that were not spoken of in this book. If you ever get confused about what to do next, just remind yourself to call on Jesus. If you ever find yourself in a horrible situation, it will be ok, all you need is to call on Jesus. WHEN YOU ARE BROKEN AND LOST AND YOU DON'T KNOW WHAT TO DO, YOU NEED TO CALL ON JESUS!

Everything you do must be Jesus, Jesus, Jesus! Jesus will take away your confusion. The Holy Spirit will reveal everything that is Jesus! Jesus is your protector, your provider, your healer, your safety, your savior, your EVERYTHING! Welcome to the new life as a believer of Jesus Christ! Everything you will ever need is in Jesus! Give him your time! Give him your energy! Jesus Christ will never leave you or forsake you! NEVER!

This book was just a taste of what God has planned for you. Move forward in your personal relationship with Jesus. Run the race set before you. Read the Word Of God and receive wisdom and revelation from Jesus Christ. Love God with all your heart, with all your soul, and with all your mind. Above all, never forget... **JESUS IS LORD!**

About The Author

James Curtis is a public speaker, minister, and author. In 2010 James had a radical encounter with the Holy Spirit. Seven years later James made it his personal commitment to preach the gospel of Jesus Christ throughout the whole world.

James's vision is to bring the body of Christ closer to Jesus in a never-ending relationship from glory to glory. James believes that the closer we get to Jesus in our personal lives, the more we can show the world who Jesus is. His teachings can be found on YouTube at James Curtis Ministries.

To contact James Curtis Ministries please email:

James Curtis Ministries

jamescurtisministries@outlook.com

NOTES

www.ingramcontent.com/pod-product-compliance
Lightning Source LLC
Chambersburg PA
CBHW071312060426
42444CB00034B/2021